DISCOVERING BIBLICAL TREASURES

UNDERSTANDING HABAKKUK

A Commentary on the book of Habakkuk using Ancient Bible Study Methods - UPDATED

Michael Harvey Koplitz

Acknowledgment

This work could not have been accomplished without Dr. Anne Davis, who taught me Ancient (Hebraic) Bible study methods, and my two study partners, Rev. Dr. Robert Cook and Pastor Sandra Koplitz. We know that the journey has just started and will last a lifetime. The discovery of the depths of God's Word is waiting for us to find.

Michael H. Koplitz

Table of Contents

Michael H. Koplitz

Introduction

While I was attending Seminary earning my M. Div. degree, I started to question what the instructors and reference books were saying about the Scriptures. One of the ideas being offered then was that the Bible was full of errors and not factual. I found that attitude disturbing for Seminary instructors to be teaching. After all, the Seminary experience is to train pastors to go out into God's world and preach the Bible. How can you preach the Bible if you believe what these instructors are teaching? The methods that were being taught to examine the Bible just seemed inaccurate to me.

After graduating from Seminary, I spent a lot of time reading different views about the Bible. I eventually read the Zohar. This collection of midrashim is considered the secret work of the Torah, according to Kabbalists. In addition, I read quite a bit about Messianic Judaism. Their view of the Bible is quite different than the Seminary view.

I decided that the biblical interpretation that was being taught in Seminary was not the biblical interpretation the people heard when Jesus Christ (whose Hebraic name is Yeshua) preached. I went on a quest to learn what the people of Yeshua's day thought about Scripture, and what they thought when the Scriptures were read. This quest led me to Dr. Anne Davis and The Bible Learning

University. Dr. Davis was in search of the same thing I was searching. She had made many discoveries that helped me in my quest. I earned the Ph. D. degree from The Bible Learning University in Hebraic Studies in Christianity concentrating on ancient Bible Studies methods.

Finally, I found someone who believed that the church has placed almost 1900 years of their theological ideas about the Scriptures and in many places possibly distorting its original meaning. What is also important to hear is that the basic tenants of Yeshua as God's Messiah, my Lord and Savior are in the Bible. My faith in Yeshua is stronger now that I have learned from Dr. Davis how to study the Scriptures in the same manner that the people did in Yeshua's day.

I have included an article that describes the differences between Greek learning methods and Hebraic learning methods. Please do not skip this chapter unless you are familiar with ancient Bible study methods because if you do then the analysis and commentary that follows may become difficult for you to understand.

Our God is vast and infinite and so is His Word. May God bless you in your discovery of what God's Word is about.

The book of Habakkuk is a vision that the prophet saw and was told to write down so that future generations would know what can happen when the people turn away from the LORD and to pagan worship. There are no historical records about Habakkuk, therefore it is difficult to determine when the book was written. Habakkuk condemns the people about the injustices, violence and ungodliness of his time. At the time of the writing the people were worshiping Baal and offering human sacrifices.[1]

---

[1] Errico, Rocco A., and George M. Lamsa. Aramaic Light on Ezekiel, Daniel, and the Minor Prophets: A Commentary Based on the Aramaic Language and Ancient Near Eastern Customs. Smyma, GA: Noohra Foundation, 2012.

Michael H. Koplitz

The main differences between the Greek method and Hebraic method of teaching

Once you are aware of the two teaching styles, you will be able to determine if you are in a class or reading a book, whether the analysis and/or teaching method is either in a Greek or Hebraic method. In the Greek method, it is automatically thought that the instructor is right because of advanced knowledge. In the college situation, it is because the professor has his/her Ph.D. in some area of study, so one assumes that he or she knows everything about the topic. For example, Rodney Dangerfield played the role of a middle-aged man going to college. His English midterm was to write about Kurt Vonnegut Jr. Since he didn't understand any of Vonnegut's books he hired Vonnegut himself to the write the midterm. When it was returned to him, the English Professor told Dangerfield that whoever wrote the paper knew nothing about Vonnegut. This is an example of the Greek method of teaching. Did the Ph.D. English professor think that she knew more about Vonnegut's writings than Vonnegut did? [2]

In the Greek teaching method, the professor or the instructor claims to be the authority. If you are attending a Bible study class and the class leader says, "I will teach you the only way to understand this biblical book," you may want to consider the implications. This method

---

[2] *Back to School.* Performed by Rodney Dangerfield. Hollywood: CA: Paper Clip Productions, 1986. DVD.

is common since most Seminaries and Bible colleges teach a Greek method of learning, which is the same method the church has been utilizing for centuries.

Hebraic teaching methods are different. The teacher wants the students to challenge what they hear. It is through questioning that a student can learn. In addition, the teacher wants his/her students to excel to a point where the student becomes the teacher.

It is said that if two rabbis come together to discuss a passage of Scripture, the result will be at least ten different opinions. All points of view are acceptable if the points can be supported by biblical evidence. It is permissible and encouraged for students to have multiple opinions. There is a depth to God's Word, and God wants us to find all His messages that are placed in the Scriptures.

Seeking out the meaning of the Scriptures beyond the literal meaning is essential to fully understanding God's Word.[3] The Greek method of learning the Scriptures has prevailed over the centuries. One problem is that only the literal interpretation of Scripture was often viewed as valid, as prompted by Martin Luther's "sola literalis" meaning that only the literal interpretation of Scripture was valid. The Fundamentalist movements of today are generally based on the literal interpretation of

---

[3] Davis, Anne Kimball. *The Synoptic Gospels*. MP3. Albuquerque: NM: BibleInteract, 2012.

the Scripture. Therefore, they do not believe that God placed any deeper, hidden, or secret meanings in the Word.

The students of the Scriptures who learn through Hebraic training and understanding have drawn a different conclusion. The Hebrew language itself leads to different possible interpretations because of the construction of the language. The Hebraic method of Bible study opens avenues of thought about God's revelations in the Scripture that may have never been considered. A question may be raised about the Scripture being studied for which there may not be an immediate answer. If so, it becomes the responsibility of the learners to uncover the meaning. Also, remember that multiple opinions about the meaning of Scripture are also acceptable if they can be supported by Scripture.

Methodology

The methodology employed is to use First Century Scripture study methods integrated with the customs and culture of Yeshua's day to examine the Hebrew and Christian Scriptures, thus gathering a deeper understanding by learning the Scriptures in the way the people of Yeshua's day did.

I have titled the methodology of analyzing a passage of Scripture in a Hebraic manner the "Process of Discovery." This methodology was developed by the author bringing together the various areas of linguistic and cultural understanding. There are several sections to the process and not all the sections apply to every passage of Scripture. The overall result of developing this process is to give the reader a framework into the ideas being presented.

The "Process of Discovery" starts with a Scripture passage. If the passage is in a poetic form, it is identified. Possible poetic techniques include: parallelism, chiastic structures, and repetition. Formatting the passage in its poetic form allows the reader to be able to visualize what the first century CE listener was hearing. The chiasms are labeled by their corresponding sections, for example: A, B, C, B', A'. Not all passages of the Scriptures have a poetic form.

The next step is to "question the narrative," which is accomplished by assuming the reader knows nothing about the passage. Therefore, the questions go from the simple to the complex. The next task is to identify any linguistic patterns. Linguistic patterns include, but are not limited to: irony, simile, metaphor, symbolism, idioms, hyperbole, figurative language, personification, and allegory.

Any translation inconsistencies discovered between the English NASB version and either the Hebrew or Greek versions are identified. There are times when a Hebrew or Greek word can be translated in more than one way. Inconsistencies also can be created by the translation committee, which may have decided to use traditional language instead of the actual translation. The decision of the translation committee can be generally found in the Preface or Introduction to the Bible.

Perhaps some of the inconsistencies were intentionally added to convey some deeper meaning therefore, the inconsistencies need to be examined.

Echoes of the Hebrew Scriptures in the Christian Scripture are identified. This occurs when a passage from the Hebrew Scripture is used in the Christian Scripture or when a command is directly discussed in the Christian Scriptures. [4] In addition, echoes can be found when Torah (Genesis through Deuteronomy) passages are used in other Hebrew Bible books. In addition to echoes, cross references are listed. A cross reference is a reference to

---

[4] Mitzvot are the 613 commandments found in the Torah that please God. There are positive and negative commandments. The list was first development by Maimonides. The full list can be found at: ttp://www.jewfaq.org/613.htm.

another verse in the Scripture which can assist the reader to understand the verse that is being read.

The names of people mentioned in the passage are listed. Many of the Hebrew names have meaning and may be associated with places or actions. Jewish parents used to name their children based on what they felt God had in store for their child. An example of this is Abraham whose original name was Abram and was changed to mean eternal father (in this case Abram's name was changed by God to Abraham indicating a function he was to perform). When the Hebrew Bible gives names, many of the occurrences will indicate something special to the reader/listener. The same importance can hold true for the names of places. The time it takes to travel between places can supply insight to the event.

Key words are identified in a verse when they are important to an understanding of that passage. There are no rules for selecting the key words. Searching for other occurrences of the keywords in Scripture in a concordance is necessary to understand how the word was being used; this must be done in either Hebrew or Greek, not in English. A classic Hebraic approach is to find the usage of a word in the Scripture by finding other verses that contain the word. The usage of a word, in its original language, is discovered by searching for the Scripture in the language of the word. The verses that contain the word being researched are identified and a pattern for the usage of the word is discerned. Each verse is examined to see what the usage of the word is which, may reveal a pattern for the word's usage. For Hebrew words the first usage of the word in the Scripture, especially if used in the Torah, is important. For the Greek words the Christian Scriptures are used to determine the word usage in the Scripture. Sometimes finding the equivalent Greek word in the Septuagint then analyzing its usage in Hebrew can be very helpful.

The Rules of Hillel for Bible understanding can be used when applicable. Hillel was a Torah scholar who lived shortly before Yeshua's day. Hillel developed several rules for Torah students to interpret the Scriptures which are referred to as halachic midrash. In several cases these rules are helpful in the analysis of the Scripture.

After the linguistic analysis is complete an examination of the cultural implications will be examined. The culture is important because it is not specifically referenced in the biblical narratives as indicated earlier.

From the linguistic analysis and the cultural understanding, it is possible to obtain a deeper meaning of the Scripture beyond the literal meaning of the plain text. That is what the listeners of Yeshua's time were doing. They put the linguistics and the culture together without even having to contemplate it. They simply did it.

This will lead to a conclusion or a set of conclusions about what the passage is talking about. Most of the time the Hebraic analysis leads to the desire for a deeper analysis to fully understand what Yeshua was talking about or what was happening to Him. Whatever the result, a new deeper understanding of the Scripture will be obtained.

The components of the Process of Discovery are:

Language
Process of Discovery
    Linguistics Section
        Linguistic Structure
        Discussion

Questioning the Passage

Verse Comparison on citations or proof text

Translation Inconsistencies

Biblical Personalities

Biblical Locations

Phrase Study

Scripture cross references

Linguistic Echoes

Rules of Hillel

Culture Section

Discussion

Questioning the passage

Cultural Echoes

Culture and Linguistics Section

Discussion

Midrash

Zohar

Thoughts

Reflections

Only the application sections are included in this document.

Michael H. Koplitz

Habakkuk – Chapter One

New American Standard 1995	Hebrew
[1] The oracle which Habakkuk the prophet saw. [2] How long, O LORD, will I call for help, And You will not hear? I cry out to You, "Violence!" Yet You do not save. [3] Why do You make me see iniquity, And cause *me* to look on wickedness? Yes, destruction and violence are before me; Strife exists and contention arises. [4] Therefore the law is ignored And justice is never upheld. For the	1 הַמַּשָׂא אֲשֶׁר חָזָה 2 חֲבַקּוּק הַנָּבִיא: עַד־אָנָה יְהוָה שִׁוַּעְתִּי וְלֹא תִשְׁמָע אֶזְעַק אֵלֶיךָ חָמָס וְלֹא תוֹשִׁיעַ: 3 לָמָּה תַרְאֵנִי אָוֶן וְעָמָל תַּבִּיט וְשֹׁד וְחָמָס לְנֶגְדִּי וַיְהִי רִיב וּמָדוֹן יִשָּׂא: 4 עַל־כֵּן תָּפוּג תּוֹרָה וְלֹא־יֵצֵא לָנֶצַח מִשְׁפָּט כִּי רָשָׁע מַכְתִּיר אֶת־הַצַּדִּיק עַל־כֵּן יֵצֵא מִשְׁפָּט מְעֻקָּל: 5 רְאוּ בַגּוֹיִם וְהַבִּיטוּ וְהִתַּמְּהוּ

wicked surround the righteous; Therefore justice comes out perverted. 5 "Look among the nations! Observe! Be astonished! Wonder! Because *I am* doing something in your days-- You would not believe if you were told. 6 "For behold, I am raising up the Chaldeans, That fierce and impetuous people Who march throughout the earth To seize dwelling places which are not theirs. 7 "They are dreaded and feared; Their justice and authority originate with themselves.	תְּמָהוּ כִּי־פֹעַל פֹּעֵל בִּימֵיכֶם לֹא תַאֲמִינוּ כִּי יְסֻפָּר: 6 כִּי־הִנְנִי מֵקִים אֶת־הַכַּשְׂדִּים הַגּוֹי הַמַּר וְהַנִּמְהָר הַהוֹלֵךְ לְמֶרְחֲבֵי־אֶרֶץ לָרֶשֶׁת מִשְׁכָּנוֹת לֹא־לוֹ: 7 אָיֹם וְנוֹרָא הוּא מִמֶּנּוּ מִשְׁפָּטוֹ וּשְׂאֵתוֹ יֵצֵא: 8 וְקַלּוּ מִנְּמֵרִים סוּסָיו וְחַדּוּ מִזְּאֵבֵי עֶרֶב וּפָשׁוּ פָּרָשָׁיו וּפָרָשָׁיו מֵרָחוֹק יָבֹאוּ יָעֻפוּ כְּנֶשֶׁר חָשׁ לֶאֱכוֹל: 9 כֻּלֹּה לְחָמָס יָבוֹא מְגַמַּת פְּנֵיהֶם קָדִימָה וַיֶּאֱסֹף כַּחוֹל שֶׁבִי:

8 "Their horses are swifter than leopards And keener than wolves in the evening. Their horsemen come galloping, Their horsemen come from afar; They fly like an eagle swooping *down* to devour.

9 "All of them come for violence. Their horde of faces *moves* forward. They collect captives like sand.

10 "They mock at kings And rulers are a laughing matter to them. They laugh at every fortress And heap up rubble to capture it.

11 "Then they will sweep through *like* the wind and pass on. But they will be held guilty,

10 וְהוּא בַּמְּלָכִים יִתְקַלָּס וְרֹזְנִים מִשְׂחָק לֹו הוּא לְכָל־מִבְצָר יִשְׂחָק וַיִּצְבֹּר עָפָר וַיִּלְכְּדָהּ׃

11 אָז חָלַף רוּחַ וַיַּעֲבֹר וְאָשֵׁם זוּ כֹחוֹ לֵאלֹהוֹ׃

12 הֲלוֹא אַתָּה מִקֶּדֶם יְהוָה אֱלֹהַי קְדֹשִׁי לֹא נָמוּת יְהוָה לְמִשְׁפָּט שַׂמְתּוֹ וְצוּר לְהוֹכִיחַ יְסַדְתּוֹ׃

13 טְהוֹר עֵינַיִם מֵרְאוֹת רָע וְהַבִּיט אֶל־עָמָל לֹא תוּכָל לָמָּה תַבִּיט בּוֹגְדִים תַּחֲרִישׁ בְּבַלַּע רָשָׁע צַדִּיק מִמֶּנּוּ׃

14 וַתַּעֲשֶׂה אָדָם כִּדְגֵי הַיָּם כְּרֶמֶשׂ לֹא־מֹשֵׁל בּוֹ׃

They whose strength is their god."

12 Are You not from everlasting, O LORD, my God, my Holy One? We will not die. You, O LORD, have appointed them to judge; And You, O Rock, have established them to correct.

13 *Your* eyes are too pure to approve evil, And You can not look on wickedness *with favor.* Why do You look with favor On those who deal treacherously? Why are You silent when the wicked swallow up Those more righteous than they?

14 *Why* have You made men like the fish of the sea, Like creeping

כֻּלֹּה בְּחַכָּה יַעֲלֶה יְגֹרֵהוּ בְחֶרְמֹו וְיַאַסְפֵהוּ בְּמִכְמַרְתֹּו עַל־כֵּן יִשְׂמַח וְיָגִיל׃ 15

עַל־כֵּן יְזַבֵּחַ לְחֶרְמֹו וְיקַטֵּר לְמִכְמַרְתֹּו כִּי בָהֵמָּה שָׁמֵן חֶלְקֹו וּמַאֲכָלֹו בְּרִאָה׃ 16

הַעַל כֵּן יָרִיק חֶרְמֹו וְתָמִיד לַהֲרֹג גֹּויִם לֹא יַחְמֹול׃ ס 17

things without a ruler over them?

[15] *The Chaldeans* bring all of them up with a hook, Drag them away with their net, And gather them together in their fishing net. Therefore they rejoice and are glad.

[16] Therefore they offer a sacrifice to their net And burn incense to their fishing net; Because through these things their catch is large, And their food is plentiful.

[17] Will they therefore empty their net And continually slay nations without sparing?

Process of Discovery

Linguistics Section

Linguistic Structure

[**Prologue**] [1] The oracle which Habakkuk the prophet saw.

A [2] How long, O LORD, will I call for help, And You will not hear? I cry out to You, "Violence!" Yet You do not save. [3] Why do You make me see iniquity, And cause *me* to look on wickedness? Yes, destruction and violence are before me; Strife exists and contention arises. [4] Therefore the law is ignored And justice is never upheld. For the wicked surround the righteous; Therefore justice comes out perverted.

B[5] "Look among the nations! Observe! Be astonished! Wonder! Because *I am* doing something in your days-- You would not believe if you were told. [6] "For behold, I am raising up the Chaldeans, That fierce and impetuous people Who march throughout the earth To seize dwelling places which are not theirs. [7] "They are dreaded and feared; Their justice and authority originate with themselves. [8] "Their horses are swifter than leopards And keener than wolves in the evening. Their horsemen come galloping, Their horsemen come from afar; They fly like an eagle swooping *down* to devour. [9] "All of them come for violence. Their horde of faces *moves* forward. They collect captives like sand. [10] "They mock at kings And rulers are a laughing matter to them. They laugh at every fortress And heap up rubble to capture it. [11] "Then they will sweep through *like* the wind and pass on. But they will be held guilty, They whose strength is their god."

A' [12] Are You not from everlasting, O LORD, my God, my Holy One? We will not die. You, O LORD, have appointed them to judge; And You, O Rock, have established them to correct. [13] *Your* eyes are too pure to approve evil, And You can not look on wickedness *with favor.* Why do You look with favor On those who deal treacherously? Why are You silent when the wicked swallow up Those more righteous than they?

A ¹⁴ *Why* have You made men like the fish of the sea, Like creeping things without a ruler over them?

> **B** ¹⁵ *The Chaldeans* bring all of them up with a hook, Drag them away with their net, And gather them together in their fishing net. Therefore they rejoice and are glad.

> **B1** ¹⁶ Therefore they offer a sacrifice to their net And burn incense to their fishing net; Because through these things their catch is large, And their food is plentiful.

A' ¹⁷ Will they therefore empty their net And continually slay nations without sparing?

Discussion

This chapter has two chiasms in it. The first chiasm is Habakkuk's words, (verses 2– 4), followed by the LORD's response (verses 5-11), followed by Habakkuk's response to the LORD's words (verse 12-13). The second chiasm is developed from the metaphor of the fishing net.

Questioning the Passage[5]

1. Who were the Chaldeans? (v. 6)

   "Chaldea, also spelled Chaldaea, Assyrian Kaldu, Babylonian Kasdu, Hebrew Kasddim, land in southern Babylonia (modern southern Iraq) frequently mentioned in the Old Testament. Strictly speaking, the name

---

[5] (The questions and answers offered are for discussion purposes. You may have different questions and answers. Remember all questions are valid and all answers must be defendable from Scripture. This applies to this section and to the Culture Section.)

should be applied to the land bordering the head of the Persian Gulf between the Arabian desert and the Euphrates delta.

Chaldea is first mentioned in the annals of the Assyrian king Ashurnasirpal II (reigned 884/883–859 BC), though earlier documents referred to the same area as the "Sealand." In 850 Shalmaneser III of Assyria raided Chaldea and reached the Persian Gulf, which he called the "Sea of Kaldu." On the accession of Sargon II to the Assyrian throne (721), the Chaldean Marduk-apla-iddina II (the biblical Merodach-baladan), ruler of Bit-Yakin (a district of Chaldea), seized the Babylonian throne and, despite Assyrian opposition, held it from 721 to 710. He finally fled, however, and Bit-Yakin was placed under Assyrian control.

With this decline of Assyrian power, a native governor, Nabopolassar, was able, in 625, to become king of Babylon by popular consent and to inaugurate a Chaldean dynasty that lasted until the Persian invasion of 539 BC. The prestige of his successors, Nebuchadnezzar II (reigned 605–562) and Nabonidus(reigned 556–539), was such that "Chaldean" became synonymous with "Babylonian."

"Chaldean" also was used by several ancient authors to denote the priests and other persons educated in the classical Babylonian literature, especially in traditions of astronomy and astrology."[6]

2. What will the Chaldeans be held guilty of? (v. 11)

In other prophetic books, this refers to the understanding that the LORD removed His protection from His people because they violated the covenant of the Ten Commandments. Therefore, the Chaldeans were able to invade Judah. The prophets called the invasion a punishment from the LORD.

---

[6] Britannica, The Editors of Encyclopaedia. "Chaldea." Encyclopædia Britannica. August 29, 2013. Accessed October 23, 2018. https://www.britannica.com/place/Chaldea.

The invaders usually did more damage and caused more suffering than the LORD had intended. Because of this overreach, the LORD promised to punish the Chaldeans for what they did.

3. What does it mean that their strength is their god? (v. 11)

The Chaldeans worshiped their strength as their god. The Chaldeans had their own false gods. They prayed to their gods, but their gods did not exist. Therefore, their strength did not come from any god. Habakkuk is saying that the strength of the Chaldeans was their god since their strength did not come from the LORD.

4. Who will the LORD appoint to judge and who? (v. 12)

   The Targum reads, "You, O God, are the true judge over all your creatures…" Therefore, it is not whom the LORD will appoint but the LORD who will judge.[7]

5. What does the simile of verse fourteen mean?

   Habakkuk says to the LORD that the LORD has abandoned His people. The LORD does not get concerned about the fish in the sea. Any fisherman can come by and capture the fish. The evil of the Chaldeans was that they could

---

[7] Cathcart, Kevin J., and R. P. Gordon. The Targum of the Minor Prophets. Collegeville, MN: Liturgical Press, 1990.

capture the LORD's people and do more damage than the LORD approved. Habakkuk is saying that anyone who can capture the LORD's people will be punished.

6. What do the references to fishing in verses 14 through 17 mean?

Habakkuk begins his metaphor of humans being like fish in the ocean in verse fourteen and continues through verse seventeen. The metaphor says that the LORD has no regard for what happens to His people. This distresses Habakkuk that it seems that the LORD has abandoned His people.[8]

8 Rashi, David Kimhi, Nosson Scherman, and Meir Zlotowitz. The Twelve Prophets. Brooklyn, NY: Mesorah Publications, 2014.

Biblical Personalities

1. Habakkuk – nothing is known about Habakkuk except that he was a prophet who wrote this book.

Scripture cross-references

Verse 8	Jer 4:13; Zep 3:3; Eze 17:3; Hos 8:1
Verse 12	Deu 33:27; Psa 90:2; Mal 3:6; Isa 10:5, Isa 10:6; Mal 3:5; Deu 32:4
Verse 13	Psa 11:4-6; Psa 34:15, Psa 34:16; Jer 12:1, Jer 12:2; Isa 24:16; Psa 50:21; Psa 35:25
Verse 15	Jer 16:16; Amo 4:2; Psa 10:9

Culture Section

Questioning the passage

1. What does the simile of verse eleven mean, "like the wind?"

   In the Middle East, "like the wind" refers to luck. It is believed that the Chaldeans had some luck when they invaded Judah. One day the wind would change and be against them. That day came when the Persians invaded and defeated the Chaldeans.[9]

2. What does it mean that the LORD's eyes are too pure to approve evil?

---

[9] Errico, Rocco A., and George M. Lamsa. Aramaic Light on Ezekiel, Daniel, and the Minor Prophets: A Commentary Based on the Aramaic Language and Ancient Near Eastern Customs. Smyma, GA: Noohra Foundation, 2012.

In the days of this writing, Semites believed that the LORD despised evil and refused to look at the faces of wicked people. He would not allow wicked people to come into His divine presence. It is evil and the sin that separates us from the LORD.[10] Therefore, Habakkuk was asking if the LORD saw the evil occurring in the Promised Land. Because it was evil, He did not take notice of it. Since the evil continued for some time, it could have been reasoned that the LORD was ignoring it.

---

[10] IBID.

Thoughts

Habakkuk put together an interesting argument about why the LORD allows evil to occur. Since evil cannot exist in Heaven, the LORD will not give a divine audience to wicked people. Therefore, it appeared to Habakkuk that the LORD did not care about evil. Habakkuk was asking the LORD how He could allow evil to occur. However, if the LORD will not recognize the evil because He does not see it, then does it exist? The LORD's answer is clear. He did indeed know about the evil and was sending the Chaldeans to destroy the evil. In this respect, it is not that the LORD removed His protection and invaded a mighty nation; instead, He was bringing a powerful enemy to clear out the evil. However, what about the righteous people who resided in the land with the wicked people? Is it fair to them to be destroyed by the wicked? This is a question that Habakkuk brought before the LORD in chapter two.

Reflections

There is so much evil in the world today that one might wonder how much longer the LORD will wait and let it continue. Could it be that the LORD does not see the evil today like Habakkuk said that the LORD did not see the evil in his day? The LORD may expect the righteous to stand up and take control. With the population of the world today and the number of nations, no nation can stand up and stop all the evil in the world. Since World War II, the United States has played the role of the police officer trying to enforce the powers of good and right. That has not worked for seventy years. Evil has infected the United States as it has in the rest of the world. Even at the local level, our worship centers have evil people in them. People call themselves good church or synagogue members who are there for themselves. They will commit any evil necessary to hold onto power within the organization. Sadly, Saint Paul established a hierarchy within the church. The minute there is the ability to have power over people, evil can infect leaders to become power-hungry evil people. This can be seen in any organization and government. It is not restricted to just religious organizations. So, where is the LORD in all of this? One day we might discover the answer to that question.

Habakkuk Chapter Two

New American Standard 1995	Hebrew
[1] I will stand on my guard post And station myself on the rampart; And I will keep watch to see what He will speak to me, And how I may reply when I am reproved. [2] Then the LORD answered me and said, "Record the vision And inscribe *it* on tablets, That the one who reads it may run. [3] "For the vision is yet for the appointed time; It hastens toward the goal and it will not fail. Though it tarries, wait	**1** עַל־מִשְׁמַרְתִּי אֶעֱמֹדָה וְאֶתְיַצְּבָה עַל־מָצֹור וַאֲצַפֶּה לִרְאֹות מַה־יְדַבֶּר־בִּי וּמָה אָשִׁיב עַל־ תֹּוכַחְתִּי׃ **2** וַיַּעֲנֵנִי יְהוָה וַיֹּאמֶר כְּתֹוב חָזֹון וּבָאֵר עַל־הַלֻּחֹות לְמַעַן יָרוּץ קֹורֵא בֹו׃ **3** כִּי עֹוד חָזֹון לַמֹּועֵד וְיָפֵחַ לַקֵּץ וְלֹא יְכַזֵּב אִם־ יִתְמַהְמָהּ חַכֵּה־לֹו כִּי־בֹא יָבֹא לֹא יְאַחֵר׃

for it; For it will certainly come, it will not delay.

4 "Behold, as for the proud one, His soul is not right within him; But the righteous will live by his faith.

5 "Furthermore, wine betrays the haughty man, So that he does not stay at home. He enlarges his appetite like Sheol, And he is like death, never satisfied. He also gathers to himself all nations And collects to himself all peoples.

6 "Will not all of these take up a taunt-song against him, Even mockery *and* insinuations against him And say, 'Woe to him who increases what is not his-- For

4
הִנֵּה עֻפְּלָ֔ה לֹא־
יָשְׁרָ֥ה נַפְשׁ֖וֹ בּ֑וֹ
וְצַדִּ֖יק בֶּאֱמוּנָת֥וֹ
יִחְיֶֽה:

5
וְאַף֙ כִּֽי־הַיַּ֣יִן בּוֹגֵ֔ד
גֶּ֥בֶר יָהִ֖יר וְלֹ֣א יִנְוֶ֑ה
אֲשֶׁר֩ הִרְחִ֨יב כִּשְׁא֜וֹל
נַפְשׁ֗וֹ וְה֤וּא כַמָּ֨וֶת֙
וְלֹ֣א יִשְׂבָּ֔ע וַיֶּאֱסֹ֤ף
אֵלָיו֙ כָּל־הַגּוֹיִ֔ם
וַיִּקְבֹּ֥ץ אֵלָ֖יו כָּל־
הָעַמִּֽים:

6
הֲלוֹא־אֵ֣לֶּה כֻלָּ֗ם
עָלָיו֙ מָשָׁ֣ל יִשָּׂ֔אוּ
וּמְלִיצָ֖ה חִידֹ֣ת ל֑וֹ
וְיֹאמַ֗ר ה֚וֹי הַמַּרְבֶּ֣ה
לֹּא־ל֔וֹ עַד־מָתַ֕י
וּמַכְבִּ֥יד עָלָ֖יו עַבְטִֽיט:

7
הֲל֣וֹא פֶ֗תַע יָק֙וּמוּ֙
נֹשְׁכֶ֔יךָ וְיִקְצ֖וּ
מְזַעְזְעֶ֑יךָ וְהָיִ֥יתָ
לִמְשִׁסּ֖וֹת לָֽמוֹ:

how long-- And makes himself rich with loans?'

7 "Will not your creditors rise up suddenly, And those who collect from you awaken? Indeed, you will become plunder for them.

8 "Because you have looted many nations, All the remainder of the peoples will loot you-- Because of human bloodshed and violence done to the land, To the town and all its inhabitants.

9 "Woe to him who gets evil gain for his house To put his nest on high, To be delivered from the hand of calamity!

10 "You have devised a shameful thing for

8 כִּי אַתָּה שַׁלּוֹתָ גּוֹיִם רַבִּים יְשָׁלּוּךָ כָּל־יֶתֶר עַמִּים מִדְּמֵי אָדָם וַחֲמַס־אֶרֶץ קִרְיָה וְכָל־יֹשְׁבֵי בָהּ: פ

9 הוֹי בֹּצֵעַ בֶּצַע רָע לְבֵיתוֹ לָשׂוּם בַּמָּרוֹם קִנּוֹ לְהִנָּצֵל מִכַּף־רָע:

10 יָעַצְתָּ בֹּשֶׁת לְבֵיתֶךָ קְצוֹת־עַמִּים רַבִּים וְחוֹטֵא נַפְשֶׁךָ:

11 כִּי־אֶבֶן מִקִּיר תִּזְעָק וְכָפִיס מֵעֵץ יַעֲנֶנָּה: פ

12 הוֹי בֹּנֶה עִיר בְּדָמִים וְכוֹנֵן קִרְיָה בְּעַוְלָה:

13 הֲלוֹא הִנֵּה מֵאֵת יְהוָה צְבָאוֹת וְיִיגְעוּ עַמִּים בְּדֵי־אֵשׁ

your house By cutting off many peoples; So you are sinning against yourself.

11 "Surely the stone will cry out from the wall, And the rafter will answer it from the framework.

12 "Woe to him who builds a city with bloodshed And founds a town with violence!

13 "Is it not indeed from the LORD of hosts That peoples toil for fire, And nations grow weary for nothing?

14 "For the earth will be filled With the knowledge of the glory of the LORD, As the waters cover the sea.

15 "Woe to you who make your neighbors drink, Who mix in your

וּלְאֻמִּים בְּדֵי־רֵיק יִעָפוּ׃

14 כִּי תִּמָּלֵא הָאָרֶץ לָדַעַת אֶת־ כְּבוֹד יְהוָה כַּמַּיִם יְכַסּוּ עַל־יָם׃ ס

15 הוֹי מַשְׁקֶה רֵעֵהוּ מְסַפֵּחַ חֲמָתְךָ וְאַף שַׁכֵּר לְמַעַן הַבִּיט עַל־מְעוֹרֵיהֶם׃

16 שָׂבַעְתָּ קָלוֹן מִכָּבוֹד שְׁתֵה גַם־ אַתָּה וְהֵעָרֵל תִּסּוֹב עָלֶיךָ כּוֹס יְמִין יְהוָה וְקִיקָלוֹן עַל־כְּבוֹדֶךָ׃

17 כִּי חֲמַס לְבָנוֹן יְכַסֶּךָ וְשֹׁד בְּהֵמוֹת יְחִיתַן מִדְּמֵי אָדָם וַחֲמַס־אֶרֶץ קִרְיָה וְכָל־יֹשְׁבֵי בָהּ׃ ס

18 מָה־הוֹעִיל פֶּסֶל כִּי פְסָלוֹ יֹצְרוֹ

venom even to make *them* drunk So as to look on their nakedness!

16 "You will be filled with disgrace rather than honor. Now you yourself drink and expose your *own* nakedness. The cup in the LORD'S right hand will come around to you, And utter disgrace *will come* upon your glory.

17 "For the violence done to Lebanon will overwhelm you, And the devastation of *its* beasts by which you terrified them, Because of human bloodshed and violence done to the land, To the town and all its inhabitants.

18 "What profit is the idol when its maker has

מַסֵּכָה וּמְוֹרֶה שָׁקֶר כִּי בָטַח יֹצֵר יִצְרוֹ עָלָיו לַעֲשׂוֹת אֱלִילֶים אִלְמִים׃ ס

19 הֲוֹי אֹמֵר לָעֵץ הָקִיצָה עוּרִי לְאֶבֶן דּוּמָם הוּא יוֹרֶה הִנֵּה־הוּא תָּפוּשׂ זָהָב וָכֶסֶף וְכָל־רוּחַ אֵין בְּקִרְבּוֹ׃

20 וַיהוָה בְּהֵיכַל קָדְשׁוֹ הַס מִפָּנָיו כָּל־הָאָרֶץ

carved it, *Or* an image, a teacher of falsehood? For *its* maker trusts in his *own* handiwork When he fashions speechless idols. [19] "Woe to him who says to a *piece of* wood, 'Awake!' To a mute stone, 'Arise!' *And* that is *your* teacher? Behold, it is overlaid with gold and silver, And there is no breath at all inside it. [20] "But the LORD is in His holy Temple. Let all the earth be silent before Him."	

Process of Discovery

Linguistics Section

Linguistic Structure

[**Action**] [1] I will stand on my guard post And station myself on the rampart; And I will keep watch to see what He will speak to me, And how I may reply when I am reproved.

[**Reaction**] [2] Then the LORD answered me and said, "Record the vision And inscribe *it* on tablets, That the one who reads it may run. [3] "For the vision is yet for the appointed time; It hastens toward the goal and it will not fail. Though it tarries, wait for it; For it will certainly come, it will not delay. [4] "Behold, as for the proud one, His soul is not right within him; But the righteous will live by his faith. [5] "Furthermore, wine betrays the haughty man, So that he does not stay at home. He enlarges his appetite like Sheol, And he is like death, never satisfied. He also gathers to himself all nations And collects to himself all peoples. [6] "Will not all of these take up a taunt-song against him, Even mockery *and* insinuations against him And say, 'Woe to him who increases what is not his-- For how long-- And makes himself rich with loans?' [7] "Will not your creditors rise up suddenly, And those who collect from you awaken? Indeed, you will become plunder for them. [8] "Because you have looted many nations, All the remainder of the peoples will loot you-- Because of human bloodshed and violence done to the land, To the town and all its inhabitants.

[Woes] [9] "Woe to him who gets evil gain for his house To put his nest on high, To be delivered from the hand of calamity! [10] "You have devised a shameful thing for your house By cutting off many peoples; So you are sinning against yourself. [11] "Surely the stone will cry out from the wall, And the rafter will answer it from the framework.

[Woes] [12] "Woe to him who builds a city with bloodshed And founds a town with violence! [13] "Is it not indeed from the LORD of hosts That peoples toil for fire, And nations grow weary for nothing? [14] "For the earth will be filled With the knowledge of the glory of the LORD, As the waters cover the sea.

[Woes] ¹⁵ "Woe to you who make your neighbors drink, Who mix in your venom even to make *them* drunk So as to look on their nakedness! ¹⁶ "You will be filled with disgrace rather than honor. Now you yourself drink and expose your *own* nakedness. The cup in the LORD'S right hand will come around to you, And utter disgrace *will come* upon your glory. ¹⁷ "For the violence done to Lebanon will overwhelm you, And the devastation of *its* beasts by which you terrified them, Because of human bloodshed and violence done to the land, To the town and all its inhabitants. ¹⁸ "What profit is the idol when its maker has carved it, *Or* an image, a teacher of falsehood? For *its* maker trusts in his *own* handiwork When he fashions speechless idols.

[Woes] ¹⁹ "Woe to him who says to a *piece of* wood, 'Awake!' To a mute stone, 'Arise!' *And* that is *your* teacher? Behold, it is overlaid with gold and silver, And there is no breath at all inside it. ²⁰ "But the LORD is in His holy Temple. Let all the earth be silent before Him."

Discussion

The LORD answers Habakkuk, telling him what would happen to the world's sinful nations.

Questioning the Passage

1. What does it mean that this writing will hasten the goal? (v. 3)

   Habakkuk's writing refers to the Messianic age and the end of time when judgment will occur.

2. Who is the haughty man? (v. 5)

   The Sages say this is a reference to Belshazzar, the grandson of Nebuchadnezzar. Nebuchadnezzar was the emperor of the Babylonian Empire when the Babylonians invaded

Judah and destroyed the Temple and the city of Jerusalem. At that time, the Temple's holy vessels were taken to Babylon. There was an incident when Belshazzar became drunk with the vine and desecrated the Temple's holy vessels. This incident caused the LORD to bring about the destruction of the Babylonian empire at the hands of the Persians.[11]

---

[11] Rashi, David Kimhi, Nosson Scherman, and Meir Zlotowitz. The Twelve Prophets. Brooklyn, NY: Mesorah Publications, 2014.

3. What does it mean that the stone walls will cry out? (v. 11)

This Aramaic idiom means that even material things would condemn injustices and oppressions.[12]

4. What does "he enlarges his appetite like Sheol, and he is like death, never satisfied" means? (v. 5)

Nebuchadnezzar had an appetite for insatiable lusts, likened to the grave and death. The wide grave was needed because his lust was so powerful. The angel of death is never satisfied and wants more souls to join Sheol.

---

[12] Errico, Rocco A., and George M. Lamsa. Aramaic Light on Ezekiel, Daniel, and the Minor Prophets: A Commentary Based on the Aramaic Language and Ancient Near Eastern Customs. Smyma, GA: Noohra Foundation, 2012.

Nebuchadnezzar continued to capture nation after nation appearing not to be satisfied with the empire that he had.[13]

5. Who are the creditors in verse seven?

The creditors are Media and Persia. These are the two enemies of the Babylonians who toppled the Babylonian Empire.[14]

6. What does it mean to place one's nest on high? (v. 9)

Nebuchadnezzar built a massive and mighty fortress in Babylon with the wood and stones of the cities he had

---

[13] Rashi, David Kimhi, Nosson Scherman, and Meir Zlotowitz. The Twelve Prophets. Brooklyn, NY: Mesorah Publications, 2014.
[14] IBID.

captured and destroyed. He used the money he stole from the people of the cities to build his fortress.[15] The fortress would have been built on a hill, so it would be difficult for an attacker to take it.

---

[15] IBID.

7. What does it mean to "cut of many people?" (V. 10)

This phrase refers to the numerous cities and nations that Nebuchadnezzar destroyed during his reign as emperor.

8. What does it mean to build a city with bloodshed? (v. 12)

This means building a city was done through oppression, confiscating property owned by the poor, and slave labor. This was very common in biblical lands.[16]

---

[16] Errico, Rocco A., and George M. Lamsa. Aramaic Light on Ezekiel, Daniel, and the Minor Prophets: A Commentary Based on the Aramaic Language and Ancient Near Eastern Customs. Smyma, GA: Noohra Foundation, 2012.

9. What does it mean to make your neighbors drink? (v. 15)

This means that one is filled with dishonor instead of glory. Also, it means that shame will cover one's glory.[17]

10. What does it mean to look at their nakedness? (v. 15)

The Sage Rashi[i] interpreted this as Nebuchadnezzar was known to sodomize the kings he captured. Alternatively, it could mean figuratively that the people's sins could be seen after their capture. In the case

---

[17] IBID.

of Judah, their sins were revealed to the Babylonians after their capture.[18]

11. What is the cup of the LORD in verse sixteen?

The cup in the LORD's right hand is a cup of curses that the LORD poured out on the people because of their sins and shame.[19] The people have exposed their shame (their nakedness), and the LORD was prepared to do something about it.

12. What does it mean to "say to a piece of wood" or "mute stone" (v. 19)

---

[18] Rashi, David Kimhi, Nosson Scherman, and Meir Zlotowitz. The Twelve Prophets. Brooklyn, NY: Mesorah Publications, 2014.

[19] IBID.

This is a warning that Habakkuk offered about worshiping idols. Idols were made of wood or stone. Many idols were covered with an overlay of gold or silver.

13. What does it mean to "let all the earth be silent before Him?" (v. 20)

The focus of prayer in ancient times was to hear and remember the voice of the LORD. The people of the Earth are told to be silent so they can hear the LORD's voice.

Phrase Study

1. וּבָאֵר עַל־הַלֻּחֽוֹת (Hab. 2:2 WTT)
This phrase can be translated as "inscribe it on tablets" or "make it

plain on tablets." The NAU prefers "inscribe." The other English versions prefer "plain or clear. The first word of the phrase can mean "inscribe or plain." The LORD wanted the vision that He gave to Habakkuk to be inscribed plainly on tablets. Therefore, those who read the vision will understand it clearly. Habakkuk was not to add any figures of speech that the reader would have to interpret. It was important for the LORD to give His message to His people clearly. In the Middle East, when something is written clearly it is said that "it can be read like water." This means that the writing moves like water, that is it is easy to read and understand and the readers will read it without stopping.[20]

Scripture cross-references

Verse 1	Isa 21:8; Psa 5:3;Psa 85:8
Verse 2	Deu 27:8; Rom 15:4; Rev 1:19
Verse 3	Dan 8:17, Dan 8:19; Dan 10:14 ; Psa 27:14; Eze 12:25; Heb 10:37
Verse 5	Pro 20:1; Pro 21:24; 2Ki 14:10; Pro 27:20; Pro 30:16; Isa 5:11-15
Verse 7	Pro 29:1
Verse 14	Psa 22:27; Isa 11:9; Zec 14:9

---

[20] Errico, Rocco A., and George M. Lamsa. Aramaic Light on Ezekiel, Daniel, and the Minor Prophets: A Commentary Based on the Aramaic Language and Ancient Near Eastern Customs. Smyma, GA: Noohra Foundation, 2012.

Verse 17   Joe 3:19; Zec 11:1; Psa 55:23; Jer 51:35

Verse 19   Jer 2:27, Jer 2:28; Jer 10:3; 1Ki 18:26-29; Psa 135:15-18; Jer 10:4, Jer 10:9, 14; Psa 135:17

Midrash

Gemara, Ein Yakov, Ta'anit 19a, says that Habakkuk dug a circular hole, stood within it, and said, "I will not budge from here until I hear what He will say to me concerning this, my question – why He looks and sees the prosperity of a wicked man." This corresponds to verse one, which says Habakkuk stood at his guard post.[21]

---

[21] The Twelve Prophets Volume Two. New York, NY: Judaica Press, 1988.

Thoughts

In the time of Nebuchadnezzar, the Judeans worshiped idols and performed different types of immoral acts, especially sexual acts. The nation that the LORD chose to invade Judah was Babylon. If the idea was that the LORD did not directly punish Judah but rather removed His protection from them because they violated the Sinai Covenant (the Ten Commandments and Torah), then it was fate that Judah's destruction would come by Nebuchadnezzar. This chapter notes that Nebuchadnezzar was never satisfied with the number of nations he conquered. He wanted to conquer the entire known world. This created enemies that he could not conquer. The Medes and the Persians would eventually take down the Babylonians. Habakkuk offers that the reason for the Babylonian empire's demise was that the grandson of Nebuchadnezzar desecrated the holy vessel of the Temple, which his grandfather took when the Temple was destroyed. Even though the holy vessels were in pagan hands, the LORD still cared about the vessels. The LORD had said that a remnant of the people would return to the Promised Land, and they would rebuild the Temple. When that time came, the holy vessels would be returned. A thought on all of this is that even the tools of the LORD are expected to be treated sacredly.

Reflections

So many churches and synagogues have been closing their doors due to a lack of attendance and membership. What happens to these buildings should concern the congregation who leaves them. Is the building sold so that pagan worship can occur or is it sold to a new group of people who want to worship the LORD? The Laurelton Jewish Center was built around the end of World War II because the town in Queens, NY, had a growing Jewish population. Unfortunately, the neighborhood changed, and the synagogue was forced to close in the early 2000's. Seeing that a Seven-day Adventist church purchased the synagogue was comforting. Why? Because the Seven Day Adventist church worships the LORD on Saturday. Of course, Shabbat worship occurs on Saturday. At least the Saturday worship of the LORD would continue. Pagan worship would not enter a former synagogue devoted and dedicated to the LORD.

Understanding Habakkuk

Habakkuk Chapter Three

New American Standard 1995	Hebrew
[1] A prayer of Habakkuk the prophet, according to Shigionoth. [2] LORD, I have heard the report about You *and* I fear. O LORD, revive Your work in the midst of the years, In the midst of the years make it known; In wrath remember mercy. [3] God comes from Teman, And the Holy One from Mount Paran. Selah. His splendor covers the heavens, And the	1 תְּפִלָּה לַחֲבַקּוּק הַנָּבִיא עַל שִׁגְיֹנוֹת׃ 2 יְהֹוָה שָׁמַעְתִּי שִׁמְעֲךָ יָרֵאתִי יְהֹוָה פָּעָלְךָ בְּקֶרֶב שָׁנִים חַיֵּיהוּ בְּקֶרֶב שָׁנִים תּוֹדִיעַ בְּרֹגֶז רַחֵם תִּזְכּוֹר׃ 3 אֱלוֹהַ מִתֵּימָן יָבוֹא וְקָדוֹשׁ מֵהַר־פָּארָן סֶלָה כִּסָּה שָׁמַיִם הוֹדוֹ וּתְהִלָּתוֹ מָלְאָה הָאָרֶץ׃ 4 וְנֹגַהּ כָּאוֹר תִּהְיֶה קַרְנַיִם מִיָּדוֹ לוֹ וְשָׁם חֶבְיוֹן עֻזֹּה׃

earth is full of His praise.

⁴ *His* radiance is like the sunlight; He has rays *flashing* from His hand, And there is the hiding of His power.

⁵ Before Him goes pestilence, And plague comes after Him.

⁶ He stood and surveyed the earth; He looked and startled the nations. Yes, the perpetual mountains were shattered, The ancient hills collapsed. His ways are everlasting.

⁷ I saw the tents of Cushan under distress, The tent curtains of the land of Midian were trembling.

⁸ Did the LORD rage against the rivers, Or *was* Your anger against

5 לְפָנָיו יֵלֶךְ דָּבֶר וְיֵצֵא רֶשֶׁף לְרַגְלָיו:

6 עָמַד וַיְמֹדֶד אֶרֶץ רָאָה וַיַּתֵּר גּוֹיִם וַיִּתְפֹּצְצוּ הַרְרֵי־עַד שַׁחוּ גִּבְעוֹת עוֹלָם הֲלִיכוֹת עוֹלָם לוֹ:

7 תַּחַת אָוֶן רָאִיתִי אָהֳלֵי כוּשָׁן יִרְגְּזוּן יְרִיעוֹת אֶרֶץ מִדְיָן: ס

8 הֲבִנְהָרִים חָרָה יְהוָה אִם בַּנְּהָרִים אַפֶּךָ אִם־בַּיָּם עֶבְרָתֶךָ כִּי תִרְכַּב עַל־סוּסֶיךָ מַרְכְּבֹתֶיךָ יְשׁוּעָה:

9 עֶרְיָה תֵעוֹר קַשְׁתֶּךָ שְׁבֻעוֹת מַטּוֹת אֹמֶר סֶלָה נְהָרוֹת תְּבַקַּע־אָרֶץ:

10 רָאוּךָ יָחִילוּ הָרִים זֶרֶם מַיִם עָבָר

the rivers, Or *was* Your wrath against the sea, That You rode on Your horses, On Your chariots of salvation?

9 Your bow was made bare, The rods of chastisement were sworn. Selah. You cleaved the earth with rivers.

10 The mountains saw You *and* quaked; The downpour of waters swept by. The deep uttered forth its voice, It lifted high its hands.

11 Sun *and* moon stood in their places; They went away at the light of Your arrows, At the radiance of Your gleaming spear.

12 In indignation You marched through the earth; In anger You trampled the nations.

נָתַן תְּהוֹם קוֹלוֹ רוֹם יָדֵיהוּ נָשָׂא:

11 שֶׁמֶשׁ יָרֵחַ עָמַד זְבֻלָה לְאוֹר חִצֶּיךָ יְהַלֵּכוּ לְנֹגַהּ בְּרַק חֲנִיתֶךָ:

12 בְּזַעַם תִּצְעַד־אָרֶץ בְּאַף תָּדוּשׁ גּוֹיִם:

13 יָצָאתָ לְיֵשַׁע עַמֶּךָ לְיֵשַׁע אֶת־מְשִׁיחֶךָ מָחַצְתָּ רֹּאשׁ מִבֵּית רָשָׁע עָרוֹת יְסוֹד עַד־צַוָּאר סֶלָה: פ

14 נָקַבְתָּ בְמַטָּיו רֹאשׁ (פְּרָזוֹ) [פְּרָזָיו] יִסְעֲרוּ לַהֲפִיצֵנִי עֲלִיצֻתָם כְּמוֹ־לֶאֱכֹל עָנִי בַּמִּסְתָּר:

15 דָּרַכְתָּ בַיָּם סוּסֶיךָ חֹמֶר מַיִם רַבִּים:

English	Hebrew

13 You went forth for the salvation of Your people, For the salvation of Your anointed. You struck the head of the house of the evil To lay him open from thigh to neck. Selah.

14 You pierced with his own spears The head of his throngs. They stormed in to scatter us; Their exultation *was* like those Who devour the oppressed in secret.

15 You trampled on the sea with Your horses, On the surge of many waters.

16 I heard and my inward parts trembled, At the sound my lips quivered. Decay enters my bones, And in my place I tremble.

16 שָׁמַ֤עְתִּי ׀ וַתִּרְגַּ֨ז בִּטְנִ֜י לְק֤וֹל צָלֲלוּ֙ שְׂפָתַ֔י יָב֥וֹא רָקָ֛ב בַּעֲצָמַ֖י וְתַחְתַּ֣י אֶרְגָּ֑ז אֲשֶׁ֤ר אָנ֙וּחַ֙ לְי֣וֹם צָרָ֔ה לַעֲל֖וֹת לְעַ֥ם יְגוּדֶֽנּוּ׃

17 כִּֽי־תְאֵנָ֣ה לֹֽא־תִפְרָ֗ח וְאֵ֤ין יְבוּל֙ בַּגְּפָנִ֔ים כִּחֵשׁ֙ מַעֲשֵׂה־זַ֔יִת וּשְׁדֵמ֖וֹת לֹא־עָ֣שָׂה אֹ֑כֶל גָּזַ֤ר מִמִּכְלָה֙ צֹ֔אן וְאֵ֥ין בָּקָ֖ר בָּרְפָתִֽים׃

18 וַאֲנִ֖י בַּיהוָ֣ה אֶעְל֑וֹזָה אָגִ֖ילָה בֵּאלֹהֵ֥י יִשְׁעִֽי׃

19 יְהוִ֤ה אֲדֹנָי֙ חֵילִ֔י וַיָּ֤שֶׂם רַגְלַי֙ כָּֽאַיָּל֔וֹת וְעַ֥ל בָּמוֹתַ֖י יַדְרִכֵ֑נִי לַמְנַצֵּ֖חַ בִּנְגִינוֹתָֽי׃

Because I must wait quietly for the day of distress, For the people to arise *who* will invade us.

¹⁷ Though the fig tree should not blossom And there be no fruit on the vines, *Though* the yield of the olive should fail And the fields produce no food, Though the flock should be cut off from the fold And there be no cattle in the stalls,

¹⁸ Yet I will exult in the LORD, I will rejoice in the God of my salvation.

¹⁹ The Lord GOD is my strength, And He has made my feet like hinds' *feet*, And makes me walk on my high places. For the choir

director, on my stringed instruments.	

Process of Discovery

Linguistics Section

Linguistic Structure

[**Introduction**] [1] A prayer of Habakkuk the prophet, according to Shigionoth.

A [2] LORD, I have heard the report about You *and* I fear. O LORD, revive Your work in the midst of the years, In the midst of the years make it known; In wrath remember mercy. [3] God comes from Teman, And the Holy One from Mount Paran. Selah. His splendor covers the heavens, And the earth is full of His praise. [4] *His* radiance is like the sunlight; He has rays *flashing* from His hand, And there is the hiding of His power.

> **B** [5] Before Him goes pestilence, And plague comes after Him. [6] He stood and surveyed the earth; He looked and startled the nations. Yes, the perpetual mountains were shattered, The ancient hills collapsed. His ways are everlasting.

C [7] I saw the tents of Cushan under distress, The tent curtains of the land of Midian were trembling. [8] Did the LORD rage against the rivers, Or *was* Your anger against the rivers, Or *was* Your wrath against the sea, That You rode on Your horses, On Your chariots of salvation? [9] Your bow was made bare, The rods of chastisement were sworn. Selah. You cleaved the earth with rivers. [10] The mountains saw You *and* quaked; The downpour of waters swept by. The deep uttered forth its voice, It lifted high its hands. [11] Sun *and* moon stood in their places; They went away at the light of Your arrows, At the radiance of Your gleaming spear.

B' [12] In indignation You marched through the earth; In anger You trampled the nations. [13] You went forth for the salvation of Your people, For the salvation of Your anointed. You struck the head of the house of the evil To lay him open from thigh to neck. Selah. [14] You pierced with his own spears The head of his throngs. They stormed in to scatter us; Their exultation *was* like those Who devour the oppressed in secret.[15] You trampled on the sea with Your horses, On the surge of many waters.

A' [16] I heard and my inward parts trembled, At the sound my lips quivered. Decay enters my bones, And in my place I tremble. Because I must wait quietly for the day of distress, For the people to arise *who* will invade us. [17] Though the fig tree should not blossom And there be no fruit on the vines, *Though* the yield of the olive should fail And the fields produce no food, Though the flock should be cut off from the fold And there be no cattle in the stalls, [18] Yet I will exult in the LORD, I will rejoice in the God of my salvation. [19] The Lord GOD is my strength, And He has made my feet like hinds' *feet*, And makes me walk on my high places. For the choir director, on my stringed instruments.

Discussion

The first verse introduces a transition telling us that what follows is Habakkuk's prayer. The A blocks are repetitive ideas because Habakkuk tells the LORD that He has heard of the LORD's punishment that made the people tremble. The B blocks are about what happens when the LORD marches through the Earth. The C block is about the power of the voice of the LORD.

Questioning the Passage

1. Where is the place where the LORD is hiding His power? (v. 4)

    This is a reference to Jerusalem. This was the place that the LORD created with His hands. It was the capital city of the Promised Land by King David.[22]

2. What does it mean that pestilence comes before the LORD and plague comes after Him? (v. 5)

When the Israelites served and obeyed the LORD, miracles were performed for them. When they disobeyed, pestilence and plagues were sent to them by the LORD.[23]

---

[22] Errico, Rocco A., and George M. Lamsa. Aramaic Light on Ezekiel, Daniel, and the Minor Prophets: A Commentary Based on the Aramaic Language and Ancient Near Eastern Customs. Smyma, GA: Noohra Foundation, 2012.
[23] Rashi, David Kimhi, Nosson Scherman, and Meir Zlotowitz. The Twelve Prophets. Brooklyn, NY: Mesorah Publications, 2014.

The Targum interprets the word רֶשֶׁף as flame. Therefore, according to the Targum, the verse says that the angel of death was sent by the LORD because of the people's sins and appears as a flame.[24]

3. What were the perpetual mountains? (v. 6)

This reference is to the King and the officials of Israel and Judah. [25]

4. What does it mean to see the tents of Cushan in distress? (v. 7)

---

[24] Cathcart, Kevin J., and R. P. Gordon. The Targum of the Minor Prophets. Collegeville, MN: Liturgical Press, 1990.
[25] Rashi, David Kimhi, Nosson Scherman, and Meir Zlotowitz. The Twelve Prophets. Brooklyn, NY: Mesorah Publications, 2014.

Cushan refers to the people who lived in Ethiopia. The distress they experienced was when they were attacked.

5. What does it mean that Midian's tent curtains were trembling? (v. 7)

Midian was invaded in the time of Moses and Joshua and defeated by the Israelites. During the period of the Judges, Midian was able to oppress the Israelites until Gideon defeated them. Midian was a nomadic people, and they did regain their strength to continue from time to time to attack Israel.

6. What does it mean that the mountains quaked, the downpour of waters, the voice, and lifting high the hands in verse ten?

The prophet is reminding the people about the wonders the LORD did for them at the bank of the Red Sea. The LORD separated the water by Moses raising his hands toward the heavens. The downpour of the waters is when the LORD brought the water upon the Egyptians who were chasing the Israelites to kill them.

7. What came in to scatter the people in verse fourteen?

This is a reference to Sennacherib, the emperor of Assyria. When the

Assyrians conquered the Northern Kingdom of Israel, they scattered the people who survived the attack into different parts of their empire. The LORD is credited with the destruction of the Assyrians by the Babylonians because of what they did to the LORD's people.[26]

Translation Inconsistencies

1. **Habakkuk 3:1** [WTT] תְּפִלָּה לַחֲבַקּוּק הַנָּבִיא עַל שִׁגְיֹנוֹת׃
[NAU] **Habakkuk 3:1** A prayer of Habakkuk the prophet, according to Shigionoth.

[NIV] **Habakkuk 3:1** A prayer of Habakkuk the prophet. On *shigionoth*.

---

[26] IBID.

[NRS] **Habakkuk 3:1** A prayer of the prophet Habakkuk according to Shigionoth.

[CJB] **Habakkuk 3:1** This is a prayer of Havakuk the prophet about mistakes:

[KJV] **Habakkuk 3:1** A prayer of Habakkuk the prophet upon Shigionoth.

[NAS] **Habakkuk 3:1** A prayer of Habakkuk the prophet, according to Shigionoth.

[TNK] **Habakkuk 3:1** A prayer of the prophet Habakkuk. In the mode of Shigionoth.

[NETS] **Habakkuk 3:1** A prayer of the prophet Habbakoum with a song.

[NOY] **Habakkuk 3:1** The prayer of Habakkuk the prophet, in the form of an ode.

The problem with the translation is the last two words of the verse: עַל שִׁגְיֹנוֹת This phrase is best translated as "in the mode of Shigionoth." The TNK version has the best translation. Shigionoth means a passionate song.

Biblical Locations

1. Teman (Hab. 3:3 NAU) – "Teman (Hebrew: תימן), was the name of an Edomite clan and of its eponym, according to the Bible[1] and an ancient biblical town of Arabia Petraea. The term is also traditionally applied to Yemenite Jews, and is used as the Hebrew name of Yemen. In the Book of Genesis, Genesis 36:15,

the name Teman is referred to a son of Eliphaz, Esau's eldest son. Job's friend Eliphaz was a Temani (Job 2:11)."[27]

2. Mount Paran – a mountain in the Sinai.

Scripture cross-references

Verse 2   Job 42:5; Psa 119:120; Jer 10:7; Psa 71:20; Psa 85:6; Psa 44:1-8; Num 14:19; 2Sa 24:15-17; Isa 54:8

Verse 4   Psa 18:12; Job 26:14

Verse 11   Jos 10:12-14; Psa 18:14

---

[27] "Teman (Edom)." Wikipedia. June 07, 2017. Accessed October 27, 2018. https://en.wikipedia.org/wiki/Teman_(Edom).

Verse 13   Exo 15:2; 2Sa 5:20; Psa 68:19, Psa 68:20; Psa 20:6; Psa 28:8; Psa 68:21; Psa 110:6

Verse 16   Dan 10:8; Job 30:17, Job 30:30; Jer 23:9; Luk 21:19; Jer 5:15

Verse 17   Joe 1:10-12; Amo 4:9; 2Co 4:8, 2Co 4:9; Mic 6:15; Joe 1:18; Jer 5:17

Culture Section

Questioning the passage

1. What does it mean that the LORD was angry against the rivers? (v. 8) The word "rivers" means "powerful nations." The powerful nations of the world at that time had rivers. Egypt

had the Nile River. Assyria was called the "land of many waters." The Chaldeans was surrounded by the Tigris and Euphrates rivers. It is believed that the later part of verse eight refers to the time when Moses and Joshua led Israel because nothing stood in their way. After all, the power of the LORD was with them.[28]

2. What does it mean that the sun and moon stood in place? (v. 11)

   People in Habakkuk's day believed that the Earth was the center of the universe and that everything revolved

---

[28] Errico, Rocco A., and George M. Lamsa. Aramaic Light on Ezekiel, Daniel, and the Minor Prophets: A Commentary Based on the Aramaic Language and Ancient Near Eastern Customs. Smyma, GA: Noohra Foundation, 2012.

around it. The Assyrians and Chaldeans believed that the sun was the center of the universe. The Assyrians and Chaldeans determined that 365 days was a year (a complete rotation of the sun). From the Israelite point of view, since the sun and moon revolved around the Earth, the LORD could stop their movement at any time.[29]

3. What does it mean that the LORD trampled on the sea with His horses? (v. 15)

It was believed that the Shekinah of the LORD came with the people when they crossed the Red Sea with Moses.

---

[29] IBID.

The horse reference is used metaphorically, meaning ascribing glory and majesty to the LORD.[30]

Thoughts

"Because I must wait quietly for the day of distress, For the people to arise *who* will invade us" (Hab. 3:16 NAU). This sets the tone for the entire book. Habakkuk pleads to the LORD to stop the sinfulness and idolatry in the land. It is difficult to understand why the people would rebel against the LORD. It is possible that since the miracles of the Red Sea and Mount Sinai were far in the past and the people forgot, they decided to take the LORD for granted. Perhaps they believed

---

[30] IBID.

that the LORD was not watching what they were doing. Habakkuk is asking for the LORD to step in but, in the end, realizes that he must wait until the LORD creates the nation that would invade and destroy the sinners. The problem is that the innocent would have to suffer also. The LORD was not going to separate the people into good and evil. However, in the book of Ezekiel, the righteous people were branded so they would not be killed. In the Gospels of Yeshua, this idea comes up. Why should the innocent suffer because of sinful people? This is a question that has been asked many times by many of the LORD's prophets.

Reflections

75% of the people surveyed in 2010, the last survey done in the United States, said they were Christians, and 1.4% said they were Jewish. That means 76.4% of the country's people say they follow the LORD. This is a considerable majority, and this majority should be elected officials that will return the country to being a Christian-Judeo nation. Why are people not voting for candidates that will change things? It is frustrating to hear the complaint about the awful things and ideas that are evolving in the United States and see that the voters are doing nothing about it. Do people not understand that when you elect non-believers in the LORD, they will create laws and make biblical things wrong? Since this is happening, the Christians and Jews will have to accept whatever punishment the LORD eventually sends. Habakkuk learned that asking for the LORD to step in and stop evil comes at a price. That price is the innocent who will also suffer. This can be stopped if true Christians and Jews are elected to our government's local, state and federal legislative and executive positions, thereby returning the nation to becoming a God-fearing nation.

Michael H. Koplitz

Endnotes

[1] Rabbi Solomon ben Isaac (Shlomo Yitzhaki), known as Rashi (based on an acronym of his Hebrew initials), is one of the most influential Jewish commentators in history. He was born in Troyes, Champagne, in northern France, in 1040. Source: https://www.myjewishlearning.com/article/who-was-rashi/.

Michael H. Koplitz

Bibliography

Davis, Anne Kimball. 2012. *The Synoptic Gospels.*

Errico, Rocco & George Lamsa. 2012. *Aramaic Light on Ezekiel, Daniel, and the Minor Prophets.* Smyma, GA: Noohra Foundation.

n.d. *Ezekiel 35 - Prophecy against Edom.* Accessed October 19, 2018. https://trumpet-call.org/2017/08/28/ezekiel-35-prophecy-against-edom/.

1986. *Back to School.* Directed by Paper Clip Productions.

Scherman, Nosson, Meir Zlotowitz, Sheah Brander and Menachem Davis. 2013. *The Prophets: The later prophets with a commentary anthologized from the Rabbinic writings.* Brookyln: NY: Mesorah Publications.

n.d. *Shame Definition and Meaning - Bible Dictionary.* Accessed October 19, 2018.

https://www.biblestudytools.com/dictionary/
shame/.

Shelah. n.d. *The Flame and the Glowing Ember.*
Accessed October 18, 2018.
https://www.chabad.org/kabbalah/article_cd
o/aid/379782/jewish/The-Flame-and-the-
Glowing-Ember.htm.